Table Of Contents

Chapter 1: Introduction to AI

What is Artificial Intelligence?

In today's fast-paced digital world, the term "Artificial Intelligence" (AI) has become increasingly popular and widely used. But what exactly is AI, and how can it be incorporated into our daily routines? This subchapter aims to demystify the concept of AI and provide practical insights on how to leverage its power in our everyday lives.

AI refers to the development of computer systems that possess the ability to perform tasks that typically require human intelligence. It is a multidisciplinary field that combines computer science, mathematics, and cognitive science to create machines capable of learning, reasoning, problem-solving, and decision-making. AI systems are designed to mimic human thought processes, enabling them to analyze vast amounts of data, recognize patterns, and make accurate predictions.

Incorporating AI into our daily routines offers numerous benefits. From enhancing productivity to simplifying complex tasks, AI has the potential to revolutionize the way we live and work. One of the most common examples of AI in our daily lives is virtual assistants like Siri, Alexa, or Google Assistant. These intelligent personal assistants help us perform tasks, such as setting reminders, answering questions, or even controlling smart home devices, just by using our voice.

AI can also be integrated into various industries, such as healthcare, finance, and transportation. In healthcare, AI-powered diagnostic tools can aid doctors in identifying diseases more accurately and efficiently. AI algorithms can analyze medical images, detect patterns, and provide early warnings for potential health risks. In finance, AI algorithms can predict market trends, optimize investment portfolios, and detect fraud. In transportation, self-driving cars are an emerging application of AI, aiming to reduce accidents and improve traffic efficiency.

Moreover, AI has the potential to streamline our day-to-day tasks. From smart home devices that can adjust the temperature based on our preferences to personalized recommendations on streaming platforms, AI can enhance our comfort and convenience. AI-powered chatbots are also becoming increasingly popular, providing instant customer support and automating repetitive interactions.

As AI continues to advance, it is important for everyone to understand its capabilities and potential. This subchapter serves as a practical guide for the general public, exploring different applications of AI and providing tips on how to incorporate it into daily routines. By embracing AI, we can unlock its power and leverage its benefits to make our lives easier, more efficient, and more productive.

Brief History of AI

The Brief History of AI

Artificial Intelligence, or AI, is a concept that has fascinated and intrigued humans for decades. In this subchapter, we will take a journey through the history of AI and explore its evolution from a mere idea to a powerful technology that is now a part of our daily lives.

The roots of AI can be traced back to ancient times, with references to artificial beings found in various mythologies and ancient texts. However, it wasn't until the mid-20th century that AI truly started to take shape. In 1956, a group of scientists convened at Dartmouth College to discuss the possibility of creating an "artificial intelligence." This event is often considered the birth of AI as a field of study.

During the 1950s and 1960s, AI research focused on developing computer programs that could mimic human thought processes. The pioneers of this era, including Allen Newell and Herbert Simon, created the Logic Theorist and General Problem Solver, which were among the first AI programs capable of solving complex problems.

In the 1970s, AI faced a period of criticism and skepticism, commonly referred to as the "AI winter." Progress in AI research was slower than expected, and funding for AI projects dwindled. However, the field experienced a resurgence in the 1980s with the development of expert systems, which could mimic human experts in specific domains.

The 1990s marked a significant shift in AI research, as machine learning algorithms became popular. These algorithms enabled computers to learn from data and improve their performance over time. This period also saw the emergence of practical applications of AI, such as speech recognition and computer vision.

In recent years, AI has witnessed unprecedented growth and advancement, thanks to breakthroughs in deep learning and neural networks. These technologies have revolutionized various industries, including healthcare, finance, and transportation. AI-powered virtual assistants, such as Siri and Alexa, have become ubiquitous in our daily lives, helping us with tasks ranging from setting reminders to answering questions.

As we move forward, AI continues to evolve at an astonishing pace. The possibilities are endless, and incorporating AI into our daily routines has become more accessible than ever. From recommending personalized content to predicting and preventing diseases, AI is transforming the way we live, work, and interact with technology.

In conclusion, the history of AI is a testament to human curiosity, innovation, and the relentless pursuit of creating machines that can think and learn like us. As AI becomes increasingly integrated into our daily lives, understanding its history and potential is crucial for everyone. By unlocking the power of AI, we can embrace its benefits and navigate the future with confidence.

Importance of AI in Today's World

In recent years, artificial intelligence (AI) has rapidly transformed various aspects of our lives, becoming an integral part of our daily routines. From smartphones and social media to healthcare and transportation, AI is revolutionizing the way we live, work, and interact. This subchapter aims to shed light on the importance of AI in today's world and how individuals can incorporate it into their daily routines.

AI has the potential to enhance productivity and efficiency in numerous fields. For instance, in the workplace, AI-powered tools can automate repetitive tasks, freeing up time for employees to focus on more complex and creative endeavors. In the healthcare sector, AI algorithms can analyze medical data to detect diseases at an early stage, improving the accuracy of diagnoses and treatment plans. AI-powered virtual assistants like Siri and Alexa have become indispensable in our homes, providing us with instant information, assisting with daily tasks, and even controlling smart devices.

One of the key advantages of incorporating AI into our daily routines is its ability to personalize our experiences. AI algorithms can analyze vast amounts of data about our preferences, behaviors, and habits, enabling personalized recommendations for movies, music, books, and even shopping. This personalization not only saves time but also enhances user satisfaction by delivering relevant content tailored to individual needs and preferences.

Furthermore, AI has the potential to enhance our safety and security. For instance, AI-powered surveillance systems can detect and alert authorities about suspicious activities, helping prevent crime. In the transportation sector, AI-enabled autonomous vehicles are being developed to reduce accidents caused by human error. These vehicles can analyze traffic patterns, predict road conditions, and make split-second decisions to ensure the safety of passengers and pedestrians.

Incorporating AI into our daily routines does not require specialized technical skills. With the increasing availability and user-friendly interfaces of AI-powered devices and applications, anyone can benefit from AI. For instance, voice assistants on smartphones can help manage schedules, set reminders, and answer questions. Fitness trackers and health apps utilize AI algorithms to provide personalized exercise and diet recommendations. Moreover, language translation apps and AI-powered language learning platforms make it easier to communicate and learn new languages.

In conclusion, AI has become an essential part of our lives, offering numerous benefits and opportunities for the general public. By incorporating AI into our daily routines, we can enhance productivity, personalize experiences, improve safety and security, and access a wide range of AI-powered applications and devices. As AI continues to advance, it is crucial for everyone to embrace its potential and explore the various ways it can enhance our lives.

Chapter 2: Understanding the Basics of AI

Machine Learning vs Artificial Intelligence

In the evolving world of technology, the terms "Machine Learning" and "Artificial Intelligence" are often used interchangeably, leading to confusion among the general public. However, it is vital to understand the distinction between these two concepts to unlock the power of AI and incorporate it into our daily routines effectively.

Artificial Intelligence (AI) is a broader concept that refers to the development of machines or computer systems that can perform tasks that would typically require human intelligence. It encompasses various subfields, including Machine Learning (ML). AI enables machines to mimic human cognitive functions like speech recognition, problem-solving, decision-making, and learning. Its objective is to create intelligent systems that can perceive, reason, and act like humans.

On the other hand, Machine Learning is a subset of AI that focuses on enabling computers to learn from data and improve their performance without being explicitly programmed. ML algorithms are designed to analyze large amounts of data, identify patterns, and make predictions or decisions based on that information. The more data the algorithm processes, the better it becomes in providing accurate results.

To incorporate AI into our daily routines, understanding the distinction between these two concepts is crucial. While AI encompasses a broader range of technologies, Machine Learning is the driving force behind many AI applications that we encounter in our daily lives. For example, voice assistants like Siri or Alexa, recommendation systems on streaming platforms, and personalized advertisements on social media platforms, all rely on ML algorithms to learn our preferences and provide us with tailored experiences.

Furthermore, Machine Learning plays a significant role in numerous industries, such as healthcare, finance, and transportation. It enables medical professionals to diagnose diseases more accurately, financial institutions to detect fraudulent activities, and autonomous vehicles to make real-time decisions on the road.

Incorporating AI into our daily routines requires a basic understanding of its underlying technologies. By recognizing the distinction between Machine Learning and Artificial Intelligence, individuals can make informed decisions about the AI-powered systems they use. It also allows individuals to appreciate the potential and limitations of AI, fostering a more responsible and ethical integration of AI into our lives.

In conclusion, while Artificial Intelligence is a broader concept, Machine Learning is a subset of AI that focuses on enabling computers to learn from data. Understanding this distinction is essential for individuals who seek to incorporate AI into their daily routines. Machine Learning is the driving force behind many AI applications we encounter daily, from voice assistants to personalized recommendations. By grasping the difference between these two concepts, individuals can make informed decisions and harness the full potential of AI in their personal and professional lives.

Deep Learning and Neural Networks

In recent years, there has been a remarkable advancement in the field of artificial intelligence (AI), specifically in the area of deep learning and neural networks. These groundbreaking technologies have revolutionized various industries and are now becoming increasingly accessible to the general public. In this subchapter, we will delve into the world of deep learning and neural networks, explaining their significance, applications, and how you can incorporate them into your daily routine.

Deep learning is a subset of machine learning, a branch of AI that focuses on training algorithms to learn and make decisions without explicit programming. Neural networks, on the other hand, are computational models inspired by the human brain's structure and functioning. Deep learning relies heavily on neural networks to process vast amounts of data, allowing machines to recognize patterns, classify information, and make predictions with exceptional accuracy.

One of the most prominent applications of deep learning and neural networks is in image and speech recognition. Thanks to these technologies, your smartphone can now identify faces in pictures, enable voice assistants to understand and respond to your commands, and even translate languages in real-time. Moreover, deep learning algorithms have been deployed in healthcare, enabling early detection of diseases, assisting in medical diagnoses, and even predicting patient outcomes.

Incorporating AI into your daily routine is easier than you might think. Personal assistants like Siri, Alexa, or Google Assistant offer valuable support by setting reminders, providing weather updates, and recommending personalized content. Additionally, AI-powered applications can streamline your daily tasks, such as organizing your schedule, managing your finances, and even suggesting personalized workout routines.

To leverage the power of deep learning and neural networks, it is essential to stay updated on the latest trends and developments. Online courses and tutorials are readily available, allowing individuals with no prior experience to learn the basics and start building their own AI models. Numerous open-source libraries and frameworks, such as TensorFlow and PyTorch, provide the necessary tools to develop and deploy AI applications.

As you embrace AI in your daily routine, it is crucial to consider the ethical implications. Data privacy, bias, and transparency are some of the challenges associated with AI adoption. Being mindful of these aspects and advocating for responsible AI practices will contribute to the development of a trustworthy and inclusive AI ecosystem.

In conclusion, deep learning and neural networks have transformed the way we interact with technology. From voice assistants to personalized recommendations, AI is becoming an integral part of our daily lives. By understanding the fundamentals and embracing AI responsibly, you can unlock the power of these technologies and enhance your efficiency and productivity.

Supervised, Unsupervised, and Reinforcement Learning

In the realm of Artificial Intelligence (AI), there are various approaches to machine learning that enable computers to learn and make decisions. These approaches can be broadly categorized into three types: supervised learning, unsupervised learning, and reinforcement learning. Understanding these concepts is crucial if you wish to incorporate AI into your daily routine effectively.

Supervised learning is akin to learning with a teacher. In this approach, the computer is provided with a labeled dataset, where each data point is associated with a specific outcome or label. The algorithm learns from this labeled data to make predictions or classifications on new, unseen data. For instance, in image recognition, a supervised learning model can be trained with numerous labeled images to accurately identify objects in new images. This approach is widely used in tasks such as fraud detection, speech recognition, and sentiment analysis.

Unsupervised learning, on the other hand, is like learning without a teacher. In this approach, the algorithm explores unlabeled data and identifies patterns or structures within it. It aims to uncover hidden relationships or clusters in the data without any predefined labels. Unsupervised learning is useful when we want to gain insights from large amounts of unstructured data, such as customer segmentation, anomaly detection, or recommendation systems. By discovering patterns, it can help us better understand the underlying structure of the data.

Reinforcement learning takes inspiration from how humans learn through trial and error. Here, an agent learns to interact with an environment and receives feedback in the form of rewards or penalties based on its actions. The goal is to maximize the cumulative reward by learning the optimal actions in different situations. Reinforcement learning has been instrumental in training AI agents for games like chess, Go, and even autonomous vehicles. It has the potential to revolutionize various fields, including robotics, finance, and healthcare.

Incorporating AI into your daily routine can range from using voice assistants like Siri or Alexa to automate tasks, to personalized recommendations on streaming platforms like Netflix or Spotify. Understanding the different types of machine learning algorithms allows you to appreciate the underlying technology behind these applications. By grasping the fundamentals, you can make informed decisions about the AI-powered products and services you choose to adopt.

AI is transforming the world we live in, and unlocking its power begins with understanding the core concepts of supervised, unsupervised, and reinforcement learning. Whether you are a student, professional, or simply curious about the potential of AI, this knowledge empowers you to make the most of the AI revolution and leverage its capabilities to enhance your daily life.

Chapter 3: Benefits of AI in Daily Life

AI in Personal Assistants

Personal assistants have always played a crucial role in helping us manage our daily lives. From scheduling appointments to organizing our to-do lists, these indispensable helpers have evolved over time to meet our changing needs. With the advent of Artificial Intelligence (AI), personal assistants have become even smarter, more intuitive, and more personalized.

AI in personal assistants refers to the integration of advanced technologies that enable these digital companions to understand, interpret, and respond to human language and commands. This breakthrough in AI has revolutionized the way we interact with our devices, making our lives more convenient and efficient.

One of the most notable applications of AI in personal assistants is natural language processing (NLP). NLP allows personal assistants to understand and respond to spoken or written language, making interactions feel more natural and conversational. Gone are the days of rigid commands and limited capabilities. Today's AI-powered personal assistants can understand context, learn from user interactions, and adapt to individual preferences.

By incorporating AI into your daily routine, you can unlock a world of possibilities. Imagine waking up to your personal assistant gently informing you about the weather, your upcoming meetings, and the latest news headlines. With a simple voice command, you can ask your assistant to draft emails, set reminders, order groceries, or even control your smart home devices. AI-powered personal assistants can anticipate your needs and proactively suggest relevant information or actions, making your life easier and more organized.

Furthermore, personal assistants can learn from your behavior, preferences, and patterns over time, providing you with personalized recommendations and tailored experiences. Whether it's suggesting new recipes based on your dietary preferences or recommending the perfect playlist for your morning jog, AI in personal assistants aims to enhance your daily routine and make it more enjoyable.

However, as with any technology, there are considerations to keep in mind. Privacy and security are paramount when it comes to AI-powered personal assistants. It is essential to understand the data collection and storage practices of the assistant you choose, as well as the steps taken to protect your information.

In conclusion, AI in personal assistants is transforming the way we navigate our daily lives. By incorporating AI into our routines, we can streamline tasks, increase productivity, and enjoy a more personalized experience. Whether it's managing our schedules, answering our questions, or assisting in various tasks, AI-powered personal assistants have become indispensable companions in our fast-paced, technology-driven world.

AI in Healthcare

In recent years, artificial intelligence (AI) has made groundbreaking strides in various industries, and one field that has witnessed its remarkable potential is healthcare. The integration of AI into healthcare has opened up a world of possibilities, revolutionizing the way we approach medical diagnosis, treatment, and overall patient care. In this subchapter, we will explore the ways in which AI is transforming the healthcare landscape and how you can incorporate this technology into your daily routine to improve your well-being.

One of the most significant contributions of AI in healthcare is its ability to enhance medical diagnostics. AI algorithms can analyze vast amounts of medical data, including patient records, lab results, and imaging scans, with unparalleled speed and accuracy. This enables doctors to make more precise and timely diagnoses, leading to better treatment outcomes. Moreover, AI-powered diagnostic tools can also help identify patterns and trends in patient data, enabling early detection of diseases and the development of personalized treatment plans.

Furthermore, AI can streamline administrative tasks in healthcare, reducing the burden on healthcare professionals and improving efficiency. Chatbots and virtual assistants powered by AI can handle routine inquiries from patients, freeing up doctors' time to focus on more critical tasks. AI algorithms can also analyze electronic medical records, flagging potential errors or inconsistencies, thereby minimizing the risk of medical mistakes and improving patient safety.

Incorporating AI into your daily routine for better healthcare outcomes is becoming increasingly accessible. Mobile health applications and wearable devices equipped with AI algorithms can monitor your vital signs, sleep patterns, and physical activity, providing valuable insights into your overall health. These AI-powered tools can help you track your progress, set goals, and receive personalized recommendations for a healthier lifestyle.

However, it is imperative to ensure the ethical use of AI in healthcare. Data privacy and security must be prioritized to protect patient information. Additionally, transparency and explainability of AI algorithms are essential to build trust and ensure that healthcare decisions are made based on sound logic.

In conclusion, AI has the potential to transform healthcare, improving diagnostics, treatment, and overall patient care. By incorporating AI-powered tools into our daily routines, we can take proactive steps towards better health and well-being. However, it is crucial to be mindful of ethical considerations and ensure that AI is used responsibly to protect patient privacy and foster trust in this rapidly evolving field.

AI in Transportation

In recent years, the field of artificial intelligence (AI) has made significant advancements, revolutionizing various industries and transforming our daily lives. One such industry that has greatly benefited from AI is transportation. From self-driving cars to intelligent traffic management systems, AI has the potential to enhance our transportation experience in numerous ways.

Self-driving cars, a prominent application of AI in transportation, have been making headlines for their potential to change the way we travel. These autonomous vehicles use a combination of sensors, cameras, and AI algorithms to navigate roads and make decisions in real-time. With their ability to detect and respond to their surroundings, self-driving cars have the potential to reduce accidents caused by human error and increase overall road safety.

AI is also being utilized in traffic management systems to alleviate congestion and improve traffic flow. By analyzing vast amounts of data collected from various sources, such as traffic cameras, GPS devices, and social media, AI algorithms can predict traffic patterns, identify bottlenecks, and suggest optimized routes in real-time. This not only helps drivers save time but also reduces fuel consumption and environmental pollution.

Moreover, AI-powered ride-sharing platforms have revolutionized the way we commute. These platforms leverage AI algorithms to match riders with drivers, considering factors such as geographical proximity, predicted travel times, and user preferences. By optimizing the allocation of vehicles, AI-powered ride-sharing platforms have the potential to reduce the number of cars on the road, ease traffic congestion, and lower carbon emissions.

Incorporating AI into our daily transportation routine can also enhance the accessibility and efficiency of public transportation systems. Intelligent ticketing systems using AI can predict demand, optimize routes, and improve the overall efficiency of public transport networks. Additionally, AI-powered mobile applications can provide real-time information about public transportation schedules, delays, and alternative routes, empowering commuters to make informed decisions and minimize travel disruptions.

As AI continues to advance, the transportation industry is poised for a remarkable transformation. However, it is important to address potential challenges such as data privacy, security, and ethical considerations when implementing AI in transportation. Ensuring transparency, accountability, and user trust will be key in harnessing the full potential of AI in this domain.

In conclusion, AI in transportation has the potential to revolutionize the way we travel, making it safer, more efficient, and sustainable. From self-driving cars to intelligent traffic management systems and AI-powered ride-sharing platforms, incorporating AI into our daily transportation routine can enhance our overall transportation experience. As AI technology continues to evolve, it is crucial for policymakers, industry experts, and the general public to collaborate in order to unlock the full power of AI in transportation while addressing associated challenges.

AI in Education

In recent years, Artificial Intelligence (AI) has made significant advancements in various fields, including education. This chapter aims to explore the potential of AI in education and how it can be incorporated into our daily routines to enhance learning and personal growth. Whether you are a student, parent, or educator, understanding the impact of AI in education can open up new possibilities and help you stay ahead in this rapidly evolving digital era.

AI has revolutionized the way we learn by providing personalized and adaptive learning experiences. Through intelligent algorithms, AI can analyze vast amounts of data and identify patterns to tailor educational content according to each individual's unique needs and learning style. This enables students to receive personalized recommendations, interactive exercises, and real-time feedback, fostering a more engaging and effective learning process.

For educators, AI can assist in automating administrative tasks, such as grading assignments and managing student records. This not only saves time but also allows teachers to focus more on providing quality instruction and individualized support to their students. Additionally, AI-powered virtual tutors can provide additional resources and guidance outside the classroom, ensuring continuous learning and personalized assistance for students.

Parents can also benefit from AI in education. With AI-powered platforms, parents can keep track of their child's progress, receive insights into their strengths and weaknesses, and gain access to personalized recommendations for supporting their child's learning journey. AI can also help parents identify potential learning difficulties or areas where their child may need additional support, ensuring timely intervention and a better learning experience.

Incorporating AI into our daily routine is not limited to formal education settings. AI-powered language learning apps, for example, can help individuals learn new languages at their own pace, with interactive exercises and intelligent feedback. AI can also enhance our daily reading habits by providing personalized book recommendations based on our preferences and reading history. Moreover, AI-powered virtual assistants can assist us in researching and gathering information, making our learning experience more efficient and insightful.

As AI continues to advance, it is essential for the general public to embrace this technology and understand its potential in education. By incorporating AI into our daily routines, we can unlock new opportunities for personalized learning, improve our knowledge and skills, and stay ahead in a world driven by constant innovation. Whether you are a student, parent, or educator, exploring the power of AI in education is a crucial step towards embracing the future of learning.

AI in Entertainment

In recent years, artificial intelligence (AI) has become an integral part of our daily lives, revolutionizing various industries and enhancing our overall experiences. One particular area where AI has made a significant impact is entertainment. From music and movies to gaming and virtual reality, AI has transformed the way we interact with and consume entertainment content.

One of the most notable applications of AI in the entertainment industry can be seen in personalized recommendations. With the vast amount of content available at our fingertips, it can be overwhelming to find something that truly resonates with our interests. However, AI algorithms analyze our preferences, viewing habits, and past interactions to provide tailored recommendations. Whether it's suggesting a new TV series based on our favorite genre or creating personalized playlists on music streaming platforms, AI has made it easier than ever to discover and enjoy new forms of entertainment.

Furthermore, AI has also been instrumental in enhancing the overall creative process in music, film, and gaming. For instance, AI algorithms can analyze vast amounts of data to create music tracks that mimic the style of renowned artists or generate background scores for movies. In the gaming industry, AI-powered characters and virtual assistants have become more intelligent and responsive, providing players with a more immersive and engaging experience.

Virtual reality (VR) is another area where AI has made significant advancements. AI algorithms can analyze user behavior and optimize VR experiences in real-time, making them more realistic and interactive. This technology has opened up new possibilities for entertainment, allowing users to explore virtual worlds, participate in thrilling adventures, and even interact with AI-powered virtual characters.

Incorporating AI into your daily entertainment routine can be simple and effortless. Many popular platforms and services are already utilizing AI to enhance user experiences. By leveraging AI-powered recommendation systems, you can discover new movies, TV series, music, and books that align with your interests. Additionally, AI-powered virtual assistants, such as voice-activated smart speakers, can provide you with instant access to your favorite entertainment content, answer questions, and even control your home entertainment systems.

As AI continues to evolve, its impact on the entertainment industry will only grow. From creating immersive experiences to providing personalized recommendations, AI has the potential to transform the way we interact with entertainment. By embracing AI and incorporating it into our daily routines, we can unlock a world of endless possibilities and enrich our entertainment experiences like never before.

In conclusion, AI in entertainment is revolutionizing the way we consume and interact with various forms of media. From personalized recommendations to enhancing creative processes and enabling immersive VR experiences, AI is reshaping the entertainment industry for the better. By incorporating AI into our daily routines, we can tap into its power and unlock a world of entertainment possibilities tailored to our unique preferences and interests.

AI in Finance

In recent years, artificial intelligence (AI) has revolutionized various industries, and the financial sector is no exception. AI has transformed the way we manage our finances, make investment decisions, and even access financial services. This subchapter will explore the incredible potential of AI in finance and how you can incorporate it into your daily routine.

One of the most significant applications of AI in finance is the development of intelligent virtual assistants. These assistants, powered by AI algorithms, can provide personalized financial advice, help you track your expenses, and even automate your savings. With the help of these virtual assistants, you can gain a better understanding of your financial health, identify areas for improvement, and make informed decisions about your money.

Moreover, AI is playing a crucial role in investment management. Traditional investment strategies are being enhanced and optimized through the use of AI algorithms that can analyze vast amounts of data in real-time. These algorithms can identify patterns, trends, and anomalies that can inform investment decisions, leading to more accurate predictions and potentially higher returns. By incorporating AI-powered investment tools into your daily routine, you can take advantage of advanced analytics and make more informed investment choices.

AI has also transformed the way we access financial services. With the rise of AI-powered chatbots, you can now interact with financial institutions effortlessly. These chatbots can answer your questions, provide real-time updates on your accounts, and even initiate transactions. By integrating AI-powered chatbots into your daily routine, you can have instant access to financial information and services without the need for a human intermediary.

Incorporating AI into your daily routine in the context of finance goes beyond just using virtual assistants and chatbots. It also involves staying informed about the latest AI-powered financial innovations, such as robo-advisors and predictive analytics tools. By familiarizing yourself with these technologies, you can make better financial decisions and stay ahead in an increasingly AI-driven financial landscape.

In conclusion, AI has the power to transform the way we manage our finances, make investment decisions, and access financial services. By incorporating AI into your daily routine, you can gain valuable insights, make informed financial decisions, and enhance your overall financial well-being. Stay updated on the latest AI-powered financial innovations and embrace the power of AI to unlock new possibilities for your financial future.

Chapter 4: Practical Ways to Incorporate AI into Your Daily Routine

Using AI-Powered Apps

In today's fast-paced world, incorporating artificial intelligence (AI) into our daily routines has become more accessible than ever before. Thanks to the advancements in technology, we can now leverage AI-powered apps to simplify our lives, increase productivity, and enhance our overall well-being. In this subchapter, we will explore the various ways you can embrace AI-powered apps and seamlessly integrate them into your daily routine.

AI-powered apps are designed to make complex tasks simpler and more efficient. Whether you want to manage your personal finances, stay organized, improve your health and fitness, or even learn new skills, there is an AI-powered app available to assist you. These apps utilize AI algorithms to analyze data, make predictions, and provide personalized recommendations tailored to your specific needs.

One popular category of AI-powered apps is personal finance management. These apps can automatically track your expenses, categorize them, and provide insights on your spending habits. By using AI algorithms, they can identify patterns and suggest areas where you can save money. Additionally, they can offer personalized investment advice based on your financial goals and risk tolerance.

Another area where AI-powered apps excel is in health and fitness. These apps can track your physical activity, monitor your heart rate, analyze your sleep patterns, and even offer personalized workout routines. By utilizing AI, they can provide real-time feedback and recommendations to help you achieve your fitness goals and maintain a healthy lifestyle.

Furthermore, AI-powered language learning apps have revolutionized the way we acquire new skills. These apps leverage natural language processing and machine learning algorithms to create personalized language learning programs. They can adapt to your learning style, track your progress, and suggest targeted exercises to improve your language proficiency.

Incorporating AI-powered apps into your daily routine can significantly enhance your productivity and overall well-being. However, it is essential to understand the underlying technologies and potential limitations of these apps. Being aware of privacy concerns, data security, and potential biases is crucial when integrating AI into your life.

In summary, AI-powered apps have become invaluable tools for the general public to streamline their daily routines. Whether in personal finance, health and fitness, or language learning, these apps offer personalized recommendations and insights to enhance your productivity and well-being. By understanding their capabilities and limitations, you can harness the power of AI and unlock its full potential in your daily life.

Smart Home Devices and AI Integration

In recent years, significant advancements in technology have transformed our homes into smart living spaces. With the integration of artificial intelligence (AI), our daily routines have become more efficient, convenient, and personalized. In this subchapter, we will explore the exciting world of smart home devices and how you can seamlessly incorporate AI into your daily routine.

Imagine waking up to a house that knows your preferred room temperature, starts brewing your coffee, and plays your favorite morning playlist. This is now a reality with AI-powered smart home devices. From voice-activated assistants like Amazon Echo or Google Home to smart thermostats and lighting systems, these devices have the ability to learn and adapt to your preferences, making your life easier and more comfortable.

One of the key advantages of AI integration in smart home devices is their ability to automate repetitive tasks. With the help of AI algorithms, these devices can learn your habits and automatically adjust settings or perform actions accordingly. For example, your smart home security system can learn your daily routine and automatically arm itself when you leave the house, ensuring your safety without any manual effort.

Furthermore, AI-powered smart home devices can enhance your energy efficiency. By analyzing your energy usage patterns, smart thermostats can adjust the temperature based on occupancy and weather conditions, helping you save on your energy bills. Similarly, smart lighting systems can automatically turn off lights in unoccupied rooms, reducing unnecessary energy consumption.

The integration of AI in smart home devices also opens up exciting possibilities for personalization. With the help of machine learning algorithms, these devices can understand your preferences, anticipate your needs, and offer tailored recommendations. For instance, a smart home entertainment system can suggest movies or TV shows based on your viewing history, ensuring a personalized entertainment experience.

However, as we embrace the benefits of AI integration in smart home devices, it is essential to consider privacy and security. With the vast amount of data collected by these devices, it is crucial to choose reputable brands that prioritize data protection and employ robust security measures.

In conclusion, incorporating AI into your daily routine through smart home devices can revolutionize the way you interact with your living space. From automating tasks and enhancing energy efficiency to personalizing your experience, AI integration offers numerous benefits. By understanding the capabilities of these devices and ensuring privacy and security, you can unlock the power of AI in your own home, making your life more convenient, efficient, and enjoyable.

AI in Communication and Social Media

In today's digital age, artificial intelligence (AI) has become an integral part of our daily lives, revolutionizing the way we communicate and interact on social media platforms. With its ability to analyze vast amounts of data and provide personalized experiences, AI has transformed the way we connect with others and consume information.

Communication has always been at the heart of human society, and AI has made it even more accessible and efficient. AI-powered chatbots have become increasingly prevalent in customer service, providing instant responses and resolving queries with minimal human intervention. These chatbots use natural language processing algorithms to understand and respond to user inquiries, making interactions seamless and hassle-free. Whether you have a question about a product or need assistance with a service, AI-powered chatbots are there to assist you 24/7.

Furthermore, AI has revolutionized social media platforms, enhancing our online experiences. AI algorithms analyze user preferences, interests, and behaviors to curate personalized content feeds. This means that your social media timeline is tailored specifically to your interests, ensuring that you receive the most relevant and engaging content. AI also helps identify fake news, spam, and malicious accounts, ensuring a safer and more trustworthy online environment.

Incorporating AI into your daily routine can greatly enhance your productivity and efficiency. Personal digital assistants, such as Siri, Alexa, or Google Assistant, use AI to perform tasks such as setting reminders, sending messages, or even controlling your smart home devices with voice commands. These assistants learn from your habits and preferences, providing increasingly accurate and personalized recommendations over time.

AI can also help you manage your social media presence effectively. Social media management tools powered by AI can analyze data from multiple platforms, providing valuable insights into your audience, engagement levels, and content performance. This information can help you optimize your social media strategy, resulting in more impactful and targeted communication.

As AI continues to advance, it is important to embrace its potential and integrate it into our daily routines. By leveraging AI-powered communication tools and social media platforms, we can enhance our online experiences, streamline our communication processes, and stay connected in an increasingly digital world.

In conclusion, AI has revolutionized communication and social media, providing us with personalized experiences, improved efficiency, and enhanced safety. By incorporating AI into our daily routines, we can unlock its power and reap the benefits it offers. Whether it's through AI-powered chatbots, personalized social media feeds, or personal digital assistants, AI has become an invaluable tool for everyone. Embrace the power of AI and transform the way you communicate and interact on social media platforms today.

AI-Enhanced Fitness and Health Tracking

In today's fast-paced world, staying fit and maintaining good health has become a top priority for many individuals. However, with the abundance of information and options available, it can be overwhelming to navigate the sea of fitness and health tracking tools. This is where the power of Artificial Intelligence (AI) comes in handy, as it can revolutionize the way we monitor and improve our well-being.

AI has the potential to transform our daily routines by seamlessly integrating with our fitness and health goals. By incorporating AI into our routines, we can optimize our workouts, track our progress, and make informed decisions to achieve our desired results.

One of the primary advantages of AI-enhanced fitness and health tracking is the ability to personalize our routines. AI algorithms can analyze vast amounts of data, including our personal metrics, preferences, and even external factors such as weather conditions, to tailor workouts specifically to our needs. Gone are the days of generic exercise plans; AI can now create customized routines that maximize efficiency and effectiveness, taking into account our unique strengths and limitations.

Additionally, AI can serve as a virtual personal trainer, providing real-time feedback and guidance during workouts. With the help of sensors and wearable devices, AI algorithms can monitor our movements, correct our form, and offer suggestions for improvement. This not only ensures that we are performing exercises correctly but also reduces the risk of injury. AI is like having a personal trainer by our side, available 24/7.

Another area where AI can significantly impact our fitness and health tracking is in data analysis. By collecting and analyzing data from various sources, such as wearable devices, nutrition apps, and medical records, AI algorithms can identify patterns and provide valuable insights. This data-driven approach enables us to make informed decisions about our diet, exercise regimen, and overall well-being.

Furthermore, AI can help us stay motivated and accountable. Through interactive apps and gamification techniques, AI can create a sense of achievement and competition, turning our fitness journey into an engaging and enjoyable experience. AI algorithms can set goals, track progress, and provide personalized rewards and incentives, making it easier for us to stay on track and achieve our fitness goals.

Incorporating AI into our daily routine is no longer a distant dream but a practical reality. By embracing AI-enhanced fitness and health tracking, we can take control of our well-being, optimize our routines, and unlock our full potential. So, why not harness the power of AI and embark on a journey towards a healthier and fitter lifestyle today?

AI-Assisted Learning and Skill Development

In today's fast-paced world, where technology is advancing at an unprecedented rate, it becomes essential to stay updated and continuously upgrade our skills. Fortunately, artificial intelligence (AI) has emerged as an invaluable tool to assist us in our learning and skill development journey. This subchapter delves into the realm of AI-assisted learning and explores how you can incorporate AI into your daily routine to unlock your true potential.

AI-assisted learning leverages the power of machine learning algorithms and advanced analytics to personalize and enhance the learning experience. Whether you are a student, professional, or simply someone looking to acquire new skills, AI can revolutionize the way you learn.

One of the key advantages of AI-assisted learning is its ability to adapt to individual learning styles. Traditional educational methods often follow a one-size-fits-all approach, which may not cater to the unique needs and preferences of each learner. AI, on the other hand, can analyze vast amounts of data to understand your learning patterns, strengths, and weaknesses. By doing so, it can tailor the learning content and pace to suit your specific requirements, maximizing your understanding and retention.

Moreover, AI-powered learning platforms can offer personalized recommendations for courses, books, and resources based on your interests and goals. Through sophisticated algorithms, these platforms can identify your areas of interest and suggest relevant content that aligns with your aspirations. This not only saves you time and effort but also ensures that you are engaged in subjects that truly captivate your interest.

Additionally, AI-assisted learning can provide real-time feedback and assessment, enabling you to gauge your progress accurately. Interactive quizzes, simulations, and virtual reality experiences can help you practice and apply your knowledge in a risk-free environment. AI algorithms can analyze your performance, identify areas that need improvement, and provide targeted feedback to help you enhance your skills effectively.

Incorporating AI into your daily routine is easier than you might think. Various learning apps and online platforms utilize AI technology to offer personalized learning experiences. By dedicating a few minutes each day to engage with these tools, you can gradually build your skills and expand your knowledge. Moreover, AI-powered virtual assistants can remind you of your learning goals, suggest new topics, and help you stay motivated throughout your learning journey.

To truly unlock the power of AI-assisted learning, it is crucial to adopt a growth mindset and embrace lifelong learning. By leveraging AI as a learning companion, you can embark on a transformative journey of continuous skill development and personal growth. So, why wait? Start exploring the AI-assisted learning opportunities available to you and unlock your full potential today!

Chapter 5: Overcoming Challenges and Concerns with AI

Ethical Considerations of AI

As we continue to witness the rapid advancement of artificial intelligence (AI) in our daily lives, it is crucial to pause and reflect on the ethical considerations surrounding this powerful technology. While AI has the potential to revolutionize various aspects of our lives, it also brings forth a range of ethical dilemmas that need careful examination. In this subchapter, we will explore some of the key ethical considerations associated with AI, aiming to provide the general public with insights and guidance on how to navigate this complex landscape.

One of the primary ethical concerns with AI is privacy and data protection. As AI systems rely on vast amounts of data to operate effectively, the collection and utilization of personal information have become inevitable. However, it is essential to ensure that individuals' privacy is respected and their data is handled securely. Users must be informed about how their data is being used and have the right to opt-out if they wish.

Another critical aspect is transparency and accountability. AI algorithms can be complex and difficult to understand, making it challenging to determine why certain decisions are made. It is crucial to ensure that AI systems are transparent, with clear guidelines on how they operate. Additionally, mechanisms should be in place to hold developers and operators accountable for any biases or discriminatory outcomes that may arise from these systems.

Bias in AI is a pressing ethical issue. Since AI systems learn from historical data, they can inadvertently perpetuate existing biases and discrimination present in that data. It is crucial to address this bias and strive for fairness and inclusivity in AI applications. Developers should regularly audit and test their AI models to identify and rectify any biases that may emerge.

The potential impact of AI on employment is also a significant ethical consideration. While AI has the potential to automate routine tasks and improve efficiency, it may also lead to job displacement. It is important to ensure that as AI is integrated into our daily routines, measures are in place to support individuals who may be affected by job losses, such as providing retraining programs and promoting the development of new job opportunities.

Lastly, the safety and security of AI systems themselves must be considered. As AI becomes more autonomous, there is a need to establish robust safeguards to prevent misuse or malicious attacks. Ensuring the ethical development and deployment of AI requires collaboration between policymakers, industry experts, and the general public.

In conclusion, as we embrace the power of AI in our daily routines, it is crucial to be aware of the ethical considerations it brings. Privacy, transparency, fairness, employment impact, and safety are just a few of the crucial aspects to be mindful of. By understanding and actively addressing these ethical considerations, we can unlock the true potential of AI while ensuring it benefits society as a whole.

Privacy and Security Risks

In today's increasingly interconnected world, where artificial intelligence (AI) is becoming a part of our daily lives, it is crucial to be aware of the privacy and security risks associated with this powerful technology. While AI offers numerous benefits and convenience, it also brings forth certain challenges that need to be addressed to ensure the safety and protection of our personal information.

One of the primary concerns surrounding AI is the potential for unauthorized access to personal data. As AI systems gather and analyze vast amounts of information, they become repositories of sensitive data, including personal details, browsing history, and even social media activities. This abundance of data poses a significant risk if it falls into the wrong hands. Hackers and cybercriminals are constantly evolving their techniques to exploit vulnerabilities in AI systems, making it crucial for developers and users to remain vigilant and implement robust security measures.

Another privacy concern arises from the ability of AI systems to process and analyze data in real-time. This real-time analysis can be highly intrusive, as it allows AI algorithms to infer personal attributes, behaviors, and preferences without explicit consent. This raises questions about the ethical boundaries of AI and the need for transparency and informed consent when it comes to data collection and usage.

Moreover, the integration of AI into various devices and platforms also presents privacy risks. Smartphones, smart home devices, and even wearable technology often rely on AI algorithms to personalize user experiences. However, this constant monitoring and data collection can erode privacy, with potential implications for personal autonomy and freedom.

To mitigate these risks, it is essential for individuals to take proactive steps towards protecting their privacy and security. This includes being mindful of the information shared online, using strong and unique passwords, and regularly updating software and security features. Additionally, it is essential for organizations and developers to prioritize data protection and implement stringent security measures, such as encryption and multi-factor authentication.

As AI continues to revolutionize our daily routines, it is crucial to strike a balance between the benefits it brings and the potential risks it poses to our privacy and security. By understanding these risks and taking appropriate measures, individuals can harness the power of AI while safeguarding their personal information in an increasingly connected world.

In conclusion, the integration of AI into our daily routines offers immense convenience and efficiency. However, it also comes with inherent privacy and security risks. Being aware of these risks and taking proactive measures to protect personal data is essential for individuals to unlock the true power of AI while maintaining their privacy and security.

Bias and Fairness in AI Systems

Introduction:

In recent years, the rapid advancement of artificial intelligence (AI) has transformed various aspects of our lives, from personalized recommendations to autonomous vehicles. AI has become an integral part of our daily routines, whether we realize it or not. However, it is crucial to understand the potential biases and fairness concerns that can arise in AI systems. This subchapter aims to shed light on these issues and provide practical insights for the general public on how to incorporate AI into their daily routines while being mindful of bias and fairness.

Understanding Bias in AI Systems:

AI systems are designed to learn from data and make decisions based on patterns and correlations. However, if the training data used to build these systems contains biases, the AI algorithms can inadvertently perpetuate and amplify those biases. For example, if a face recognition AI system is trained using predominantly male faces, it may perform poorly in recognizing female faces. It is essential to be aware of these biases to ensure fairness and avoid discrimination.

Ensuring Fairness in AI Systems:

To incorporate AI into our daily routines while promoting fairness, it is essential to consider several key factors. Firstly, diverse representation in the development of AI systems is crucial. Encouraging diverse teams with different perspectives can help identify and address biases more effectively. Secondly, thorough testing and evaluation of AI systems are necessary to identify and mitigate any biases that may have been inadvertently introduced.

Transparency and Explainability:

AI systems often operate as black boxes, making it difficult to understand how they arrive at their decisions. This lack of transparency can be problematic when it comes to identifying and rectifying biases. Therefore, efforts should be made to develop AI systems that are transparent and explainable, allowing users to understand the reasoning behind the decisions made by these systems.

The Role of Regulation:

In addition to individual efforts, regulatory bodies play a crucial role in ensuring fairness in AI systems. Governments and organizations should establish guidelines and regulations to promote transparency, accountability, and ethical use of AI. These regulations can help safeguard against biased decision-making and mitigate any potential harm caused by AI systems.

Conclusion:

As AI becomes increasingly integrated into our daily routines, it is important to be aware of the biases and fairness concerns associated with these systems. By understanding the potential pitfalls and taking proactive measures, we can maximize the benefits of AI while minimizing the risks. Promoting diversity, transparency, and regulation are key steps towards achieving fair and unbiased AI systems. By incorporating these principles into our daily lives, we can unlock the full power of AI while ensuring a fair and equitable future for all.

Unemployment and Job Displacement

In today's rapidly evolving world, the integration of artificial intelligence (AI) into various aspects of our lives has become increasingly prevalent. As AI continues to advance, it is crucial for the general public to understand the impact it can have on employment and job displacement. This subchapter aims to shed light on these concerns and provide insights on how to navigate this changing landscape.

Unemployment, the state of being without a job, is a pressing issue that affects individuals and societies worldwide. AI, with its ability to automate tasks and processes, has the potential to disrupt traditional job markets. Many fear that AI will replace human workers, leading to higher unemployment rates. While it is true that certain industries may see a decline in job opportunities, it is essential to recognize that AI also brings forth new possibilities and creates entirely new job roles.

Job displacement, on the other hand, refers to the situation where individuals find themselves out of work due to the adoption of AI and automation technologies. This displacement can be challenging, but it also presents an opportunity for individuals to reskill and adapt to the changing job market. As AI takes over repetitive and mundane tasks, it allows workers to focus on more creative and complex aspects of their job, ultimately enhancing productivity and job satisfaction.

To incorporate AI into our daily routines, it is crucial to foster a proactive mindset. Individuals should embrace lifelong learning and seek opportunities to upskill or reskill themselves. By acquiring new skills, such as data analysis, programming, or problem-solving, individuals can position themselves to excel in the AI-driven job market. Additionally, governments, educational institutions, and organizations must collaborate to provide accessible and affordable training programs to help workers transition into new roles effectively.

Furthermore, it is essential for individuals to stay informed about AI advancements and their potential impact on their respective industries. By staying up-to-date with the latest trends and developments, individuals can anticipate changes and take proactive measures to adapt their skill sets accordingly.

In conclusion, while AI can bring about concerns regarding unemployment and job displacement, it is crucial to approach this technology with a proactive mindset. By embracing lifelong learning, staying informed, and acquiring new skills, individuals can tap into the power of AI and unlock new opportunities.

With the right approach, AI can enhance our daily routines and contribute to a more productive and fulfilling future.

Transparency and Explainability in AI Systems

In recent years, artificial intelligence (AI) has become an integral part of our lives, transforming the way we live, work, and interact with technology. From voice assistants like Siri and Alexa to personalized recommendations on streaming platforms, AI is everywhere. As AI continues to advance and permeate various aspects of our daily routine, it is crucial to understand the importance of transparency and explainability in AI systems.

Transparency refers to the ability to understand and interpret how AI systems make decisions or arrive at certain outcomes. It is essential for users to be able to trust and comprehend the logic behind AI algorithms. Without transparency, AI systems can become a black box, making it challenging to uncover biases, errors, or unethical practices.

Explainability, on the other hand, goes beyond transparency by providing clear and meaningful explanations for AI-generated outputs. It ensures that users can comprehend why a particular decision was made by an AI system. Explainability is particularly critical when AI systems are employed in high-stakes domains such as healthcare, finance, or criminal justice.

To incorporate AI into your daily routine while ensuring transparency and explainability, there are a few key considerations to keep in mind. Firstly, it is crucial to choose AI systems that are designed with transparency and explainability in mind. Look for platforms or applications that provide detailed information about their algorithms, data sources, and decision-making processes. This will help you understand how the AI system works and whether it aligns with your values and expectations.

Additionally, pay attention to the data being used by AI systems. Biased or incomplete data can lead to biased outcomes, perpetuating unfair or discriminatory practices. Demand that AI systems rely on diverse and representative datasets to avoid reinforcing existing biases or inequalities.

Furthermore, as a user, it is essential to actively question and critically evaluate the decisions made by AI systems. If an AI-generated recommendation seems questionable or raises concerns, don't hesitate to seek clarification or alternative solutions. Engaging in a dialogue with AI systems' developers, service providers, or other users can contribute to improving transparency and explainability.

Lastly, policymakers and organizations need to prioritize transparency and explainability in AI systems by implementing regulations and guidelines. Transparency should not solely rely on the responsibility of users, but rather be a fundamental requirement for AI systems' developers and providers.

In conclusion, incorporating AI into your daily routine can bring numerous benefits, but it is crucial to ensure transparency and explainability in AI systems. By demanding transparency, evaluating data quality, questioning decisions, and advocating for regulations, we can unlock the power of AI while maintaining control, trust, and ethical practices.

Chapter 6: How to Stay Informed and Updated on AI Developments

Trusted Sources for AI News and Information

In the fast-paced world of artificial intelligence (AI), staying up-to-date with the latest news and information is crucial to understanding the potential impact it can have on our daily lives. However, with the abundance of resources available, it can be overwhelming to determine which sources are reliable and trustworthy. In this subchapter, we will explore some of the most trusted sources for AI news and information, ensuring that you can make informed decisions about incorporating AI into your daily routine.

1. AI Research Institutions and Universities:
Leading research institutions and universities are at the forefront of AI advancements. Institutions such as MIT, Stanford University, and Oxford University have dedicated departments and research centers focused on AI. They often publish cutting-edge research papers and host conferences where experts share their insights. Keeping an eye on their publications and attending their events can provide valuable and reliable information about the latest developments in AI.

2. Industry Publications and Journals:
Several reputable publications and journals exist that focus on AI and its applications. Publications like MIT Technology Review, IEEE Spectrum, and The Verge have dedicated sections covering AI news, breakthroughs, and analysis. These sources employ journalists and experts who thoroughly research and fact-check their articles, ensuring the information they provide is accurate and reliable.

3. AI Blogs and Podcasts:
There are numerous AI-focused blogs and podcasts that cater to both experts and general audiences. Blogs like Towards Data Science, AI Trends, and AI

News provide insights into the world of AI from industry professionals and experts. Podcasts like the "AI Alignment Podcast" and "The AI Alignment Newsletter" delve into the ethical and societal aspects of AI. These platforms offer a more accessible and conversational approach to learning about AI, making them suitable for incorporating AI into your daily routine.

4. AI Conferences and Events:
Attending AI conferences and events provides an excellent opportunity to hear from industry leaders and experts firsthand. Events like the International Conference on Machine Learning (ICML), NeurIPS, and AI Expo bring together researchers, developers, and enthusiasts under one roof. These events often feature keynote speeches, panel discussions, and workshops that cover a wide range of AI topics, enabling you to expand your knowledge and network with like-minded individuals.

By relying on trusted sources for AI news and information, you can ensure that you are well-informed about the latest advancements and trends in this rapidly evolving field. Incorporating AI into your daily routine becomes easier when you have access to reliable information from reputable sources. Stay curious, explore these sources, and unlock the power of AI in your life.

Online Communities and Forums

In today's digital age, technology has become deeply ingrained in our daily lives. Artificial Intelligence (AI), in particular, has rapidly transformed various industries and sectors. From healthcare to finance, AI has proven to be a powerful tool that enhances efficiency and productivity. But what about incorporating AI into our daily routines as individuals? This subchapter will explore the role of online communities and forums in unlocking the power of AI for the general public.

Online communities and forums have emerged as virtual spaces where individuals can connect, collaborate, and share their knowledge and experiences. These platforms offer a unique opportunity for people to explore and learn about AI, even if they have no prior technical background. By joining these communities, you can tap into a wealth of information and resources related to AI, enabling you to incorporate this transformative technology into your daily routine.

One of the primary benefits of online communities and forums is the ability to engage in discussions with like-minded individuals. Whether you are a tech enthusiast or a complete beginner, these platforms provide a safe and welcoming environment for asking questions, seeking advice, and sharing insights. By actively participating in these discussions, you can gain valuable insights from experts, learn about AI use cases, and discover innovative ways to integrate AI into your daily life.

Moreover, online communities and forums often host webinars, workshops, and tutorials, which are designed to educate and empower individuals in their AI journey. These resources can help you understand the fundamentals of AI, explore its applications in different domains, and learn how to leverage AI tools and platforms effectively. With these newfound skills and knowledge, you can start incorporating AI into your daily routine in practical and meaningful ways.

Furthermore, online communities and forums serve as a platform for sharing success stories and real-world examples of how AI has revolutionized various aspects of life. By hearing about others' experiences, you can gain inspiration and ideas for incorporating AI into your own routines. Whether it's using AI-powered virtual assistants to streamline your tasks or leveraging AI algorithms to improve your personal finance management, the possibilities are endless.

In conclusion, online communities and forums play a pivotal role in unlocking the power of AI for the general public. By joining these virtual spaces, you can connect with like-minded individuals, access valuable resources, and learn from experts in the field. These platforms offer a unique opportunity to explore the world of AI and discover innovative ways to incorporate this transformative technology into your daily routine. So, don't hesitate to join these communities and embark on your AI journey today!

Attending AI Conferences and Events

In today's fast-paced world, artificial intelligence (AI) has become an integral part of our lives. From voice assistants to recommendation algorithms, AI is revolutionizing the way we interact with technology. If you are interested in incorporating AI into your daily routine, attending AI conferences and events can be a tremendous opportunity to learn, network, and stay updated with the latest trends in this rapidly evolving field.

AI conferences and events bring together experts, researchers, and enthusiasts from various industries, making them an ideal platform for knowledge sharing and collaboration. These events offer a unique chance to delve deep into the world of AI, gain insights from industry leaders, and discover practical applications that can enhance your daily life.

One of the key benefits of attending AI conferences and events is the opportunity to learn from renowned experts. These conferences often feature keynote speeches, panel discussions, and workshops led by experts who have made significant contributions to the field of AI. By attending these sessions, you can gain valuable insights into the latest advancements, emerging technologies, and best practices for incorporating AI into your daily routine.

Moreover, AI conferences and events provide an excellent networking opportunity. You can connect with like-minded individuals who share your passion for AI and exchange ideas and experiences. Networking at these events can lead to collaborations, partnerships, and even job opportunities. It is an opportunity to build relationships with industry professionals and experts, which can further enrich your understanding of AI and its applications.

Additionally, AI conferences and events often showcase cutting-edge technologies and products. From AI-powered devices to innovative software solutions, you can explore the latest tools and technologies that can simplify and enhance your daily tasks. These events also allow you to interact with exhibitors, ask questions, and get hands-on experience with AI-powered products.

Attending AI conferences and events is not limited to experts or professionals in the field. As a member of the general public, you can benefit immensely from these gatherings. They provide a platform for individuals from all backgrounds and knowledge levels to learn, explore, and embrace the power of AI in their daily lives.

In conclusion, attending AI conferences and events is a fantastic way to unlock the power of AI and incorporate it into your daily routine. These events provide opportunities to learn from experts, network with like-minded individuals, and explore the latest technologies. Whether you are a beginner or an AI enthusiast, attending these events will undoubtedly expand your knowledge and open doors to new possibilities. So, mark your calendars and prepare to immerse yourself in the fascinating world of AI at the next conference or event near you!

Continuous Learning and Skill Development

In today's rapidly evolving world, the integration of Artificial Intelligence (AI) into our daily lives has become inevitable. AI has the potential to transform the way we live, work, and interact with technology. To fully harness the power of AI, it is essential for the general public to embrace continuous learning and skill development.

Continuous learning is the key to staying updated with the latest advancements in AI and ensuring that we can effectively incorporate it into our daily routines. By dedicating time and effort towards learning about AI, we can better understand its capabilities, limitations, and potential applications. This knowledge empowers us to make informed decisions and leverage AI to improve various aspects of our lives.

Skill development is equally important to effectively incorporate AI into our daily routines. As AI technologies continue to advance, new skills and competencies will be required to maximize their potential. By investing in skill development, we can stay ahead of the curve and adapt to the changing demands of the AI-driven world.

There are several ways in which individuals can engage in continuous learning and skill development related to AI. Online courses, webinars, and workshops offer opportunities to learn about AI concepts, algorithms, and applications. Many universities and educational institutions also offer specialized AI programs and degrees for those looking to gain in-depth knowledge.

Additionally, staying updated with AI news, research papers, and industry trends through online platforms and social media can help individuals stay informed about the latest developments in the field. Engaging in discussions and participating in AI-focused communities can provide valuable insights and foster a collaborative learning environment.

Incorporating AI into our daily routines requires not only technical knowledge but also an understanding of ethical considerations and societal implications. As AI becomes increasingly integrated into various domains, it is crucial to develop a well-rounded perspective on its impact and implications.

Continuous learning and skill development in AI can open up new opportunities, enhance problem-solving abilities, and enable us to make informed decisions in an AI-driven world. By embracing the power of AI and dedicating ourselves to continuous learning, we can unlock its full potential and shape a future where AI enhances our lives in meaningful and transformative ways.

Remember, AI is not just for experts or tech enthusiasts – it is for everyone. Start your journey today by exploring the vast resources available and join the growing community of individuals who are harnessing the power of AI to create a better future for all.

Chapter 7: Future Possibilities and Impact of AI

AI in Robotics and Automation

In recent years, the field of robotics and automation has undergone a significant transformation, thanks to the advancements in Artificial Intelligence (AI) technology. AI has revolutionized the way we perceive and interact with robots, making them more intelligent, adaptable, and capable of performing complex tasks. This subchapter aims to explore the role of AI in robotics and automation, and how it can be incorporated into our daily routines.

AI-powered robots have the potential to revolutionize industries across the board, from manufacturing and healthcare to transportation and agriculture. These intelligent machines are equipped with sensors, cameras, and advanced algorithms that enable them to perceive and understand the world around them. By combining AI with robotics, machines can adapt to dynamic environments, learn from data, and make informed decisions in real-time.

One of the most significant benefits of AI in robotics and automation is its ability to improve efficiency and productivity. Robots can perform repetitive and mundane tasks with precision and accuracy, reducing human error and increasing output. This allows humans to focus on more creative and complex tasks, ultimately enhancing overall productivity. For example, in manufacturing, AI-powered robots can assemble products at a much faster rate, ensuring high-quality and consistent results.

Incorporating AI into our daily routines can also have a significant impact on our personal lives. Smart home devices, such as voice assistants and automated cleaning robots, have become increasingly popular. These devices utilize AI algorithms to understand and respond to human commands, making our lives more convenient and efficient. AI-powered personal assistants can schedule appointments, remind us of important tasks, and even provide personalized recommendations based on our preferences.

Moreover, AI in robotics and automation has the potential to address some of the pressing challenges we face as a society. For instance, in healthcare, AI-powered robots can assist in surgeries, analyze medical images, and provide personalized care to patients. This not only improves the accuracy of medical diagnoses but also enhances patient outcomes and reduces healthcare costs.

In conclusion, AI in robotics and automation has the power to transform industries, improve efficiency, and enhance our daily lives. The integration of AI technology into robots enables them to perform complex tasks, adapt to dynamic environments, and make intelligent decisions. From manufacturing to healthcare and personal devices, AI has the potential to revolutionize the way we work, live, and interact with machines. As AI continues to evolve, it is crucial for individuals to explore and embrace the possibilities it offers, as it has the potential to unlock a world of endless opportunities for everyone.

AI in Space Exploration

The realm of space exploration has always fascinated humankind, with its mysteries and potential for scientific discovery. In recent years, there has been a significant breakthrough in our ability to explore space, thanks to the integration of Artificial Intelligence (AI) technologies. AI is revolutionizing the way we approach space missions, making them more efficient, cost-effective, and safer than ever before. In this subchapter, we will explore the incredible impact of AI in space exploration and how it is transforming our understanding of the universe.

One of the key areas where AI has made a profound difference is in autonomous spacecraft navigation. Traditionally, spacecraft relied heavily on human intervention for navigation, which posed limitations on the distance they could cover and the tasks they could perform. However, with AI, spacecraft can now navigate through the vastness of space with minimal human intervention. AI algorithms enable spacecraft to analyze and interpret complex data from various sensors, allowing them to make intelligent decisions in real-time. This capability has opened up new possibilities for deep space exploration, where human intervention is impractical or impossible.

Another area where AI has proven invaluable is in data analysis. Space missions generate an enormous amount of data that is often overwhelming for human scientists to process and understand. AI algorithms can sift through this data, identifying patterns, anomalies, and insights that would otherwise go unnoticed. By leveraging AI, scientists can accelerate their research and make groundbreaking discoveries in a fraction of the time it would take using traditional methods.

Furthermore, AI has been instrumental in enhancing the safety and reliability of space missions. AI-powered systems can predict and mitigate potential risks by continuously monitoring spacecraft health, detecting anomalies, and suggesting corrective actions. This proactive approach minimizes the chances of system failures and ensures the well-being of astronauts during long-duration missions.

In conclusion, AI is transforming space exploration by revolutionizing spacecraft navigation, enabling efficient data analysis, and enhancing mission safety. The integration of AI technologies has opened up new frontiers in deep space exploration, allowing us to delve deeper into the mysteries of the universe. As AI continues to advance, we can expect even greater breakthroughs in our understanding of space, paving the way for future generations to explore and conquer the unknown.

AI in Climate Change Solutions

Climate change is one of the most pressing challenges of our time. As the earth's temperature continues to rise and extreme weather events become more frequent, finding effective solutions to combat climate change is crucial. Thankfully, advancements in technology, specifically artificial intelligence (AI), offer immense potential in addressing this global crisis.

AI has the power to revolutionize the way we tackle climate change by providing innovative solutions and insights that were previously unimaginable. This subchapter explores the various ways in which AI can be incorporated into our daily lives to combat climate change.

One of the key areas where AI can make a significant impact is in energy management. By analyzing vast amounts of data, AI algorithms can optimize energy consumption, reduce waste, and improve the efficiency of energy grids. Smart home devices, such as AI-powered thermostats, can learn our behavior patterns and adjust temperature settings accordingly, leading to substantial energy savings. Similarly, AI can optimize renewable energy generation by predicting weather patterns and adjusting output accordingly.

Transportation is another sector where AI can play a vital role in reducing carbon emissions. Intelligent traffic management systems can optimize traffic flow, reducing congestion and emissions. AI can also help in the development and deployment of electric and autonomous vehicles, making transportation more sustainable and efficient.

AI can also aid in the monitoring and management of natural resources. By analyzing satellite imagery and sensor data, AI algorithms can detect deforestation, illegal logging, and pollution in real-time, enabling swift interventions. Additionally, AI can assist in precision agriculture, optimizing water and fertilizer usage, and reducing chemical inputs.

Furthermore, AI can facilitate climate modeling and prediction. By analyzing historical climate data, AI algorithms can forecast future climate scenarios, helping policymakers and scientists make informed decisions. This technology can also aid in predicting extreme weather events, providing early warnings and enabling timely evacuations and disaster preparedness.

In conclusion, incorporating AI into our daily routines can have a profound impact on combating climate change. From energy management to transportation and resource monitoring, AI offers innovative solutions that can help us build a sustainable future. By embracing AI technologies and leveraging their potential, we can collectively contribute to mitigating the effects of climate change and preserving our planet for future generations.

AI in Personalized Medicine

Personalized medicine is a revolutionary approach that tailors medical treatments to individual patients based on their unique characteristics. It takes into account a person's genetic makeup, lifestyle, and environmental factors to deliver precise and effective therapies. With the rapid advancements in artificial intelligence (AI), personalized medicine is poised to revolutionize healthcare like never before.

AI has the potential to transform the way we diagnose, treat, and prevent diseases. By analyzing vast amounts of data, AI algorithms can identify patterns and insights that may be impossible for humans to detect. This enables healthcare professionals to make more accurate predictions, provide targeted interventions, and ultimately improve patient outcomes.

Incorporating AI into personalized medicine has several benefits for the general public. First and foremost, it allows for early detection and diagnosis of diseases. AI algorithms can analyze a person's medical history, genetic information, and lifestyle data to identify potential health risks. This proactive approach enables individuals to take preventive measures and make necessary lifestyle changes to reduce the likelihood of developing certain diseases.

Furthermore, AI can assist physicians in creating personalized treatment plans. By leveraging AI, doctors can consider an individual's unique characteristics and predict the most effective therapies for a specific patient. This eliminates the trial-and-error approach often seen in traditional medicine and reduces the risk of adverse reactions or ineffective treatments.

AI in personalized medicine also has the potential to improve medication management. AI algorithms can analyze a person's response to medication, predict potential side effects, and optimize dosages for maximum efficacy. This ensures that patients receive the right medication at the right dose, minimizing the likelihood of complications or adverse reactions.

Additionally, AI can play a significant role in advancing research and drug development. By analyzing vast amounts of medical data, AI algorithms can identify new drug targets, predict drug responses, and accelerate the discovery of novel therapies. This holds great promise for the development of personalized treatments for diseases that currently have limited options.

Incorporating AI into your daily routine for personalized medicine can be as simple as utilizing health apps and wearable devices that collect and analyze your health data. These tools can provide valuable insights into your overall well-being, alert you to potential health risks, and suggest personalized lifestyle changes to improve your health.

In conclusion, AI in personalized medicine is transforming healthcare by providing more accurate diagnoses, targeted treatments, and improved patient outcomes. By incorporating AI into our daily routines through various health technologies, we can take charge of our health and make informed decisions to prevent diseases, optimize treatments, and live healthier lives.

AI in Decision-Making and Problem Solving

In today's fast-paced world, where information overload can often overwhelm us, artificial intelligence (AI) has emerged as a powerful tool to aid decision-making and problem-solving processes. From personal tasks to professional endeavors, AI has the potential to revolutionize how we incorporate it into our daily routines.

One of the key benefits of AI in decision-making is its ability to process vast amounts of data in a fraction of the time it would take for a human to do so. By using algorithms and machine learning techniques, AI systems can analyze complex data sets, identify patterns, and make informed predictions. This means that AI can help us make more accurate and efficient decisions in both personal and professional contexts.

For instance, in our personal lives, AI-powered personal assistants like Siri and Alexa have become indispensable. These voice-activated assistants can help us manage our schedules, provide recommendations for restaurants or movies, and even control our smart homes. By learning from our preferences and behaviors, these AI systems can make suggestions tailored to our specific needs and desires.

AI is also transforming the world of business. From supply chain management to customer service, AI-powered applications are helping organizations streamline their operations and drive growth. For example, AI algorithms can analyze customer data to identify trends and preferences, allowing businesses to offer personalized experiences and targeted marketing campaigns.

When it comes to problem-solving, AI can be a game-changer. AI systems can analyze complex problems, break them down into smaller components, and propose solutions based on historical data and patterns. This can be particularly helpful in fields like healthcare, finance, and engineering, where complex problems often require innovative solutions.

However, as we embrace AI in our daily routines, it is essential to understand its limitations. AI systems are only as good as the data they are trained on, and biases in the data can lead to biased outcomes. Additionally, AI lacks human intuition and creativity, which are often critical in certain decision-making scenarios.

In conclusion, AI has the potential to unlock new possibilities in decision-making and problem-solving for the general public. By incorporating AI into our daily routines, we can harness its power to make more informed decisions, save time and resources, and drive innovation. However, it is crucial to be aware of the limitations and ethical considerations associated with AI. As AI continues to evolve, it is up to us to harness its power responsibly and ensure that it benefits society as a whole.

Chapter 8: The Ethical Responsibility of AI Users

Ensuring Ethical Usage of AI

As artificial intelligence (AI) continues to transform various aspects of our daily lives, it is crucial to ensure its ethical usage. AI has the potential to revolutionize the way we live, work, and interact with technology, but it also comes with a range of challenges and concerns. This subchapter aims to provide the general public with insights on how to incorporate AI into their daily routines while upholding ethical principles.

First and foremost, it is essential to understand the ethical implications of AI. AI systems are designed to learn and make decisions based on vast amounts of data, which raises concerns about potential biases and discrimination. As a responsible user of AI, it is important to be aware of these biases and actively work to mitigate them. This can be achieved by using diverse and representative datasets, regularly monitoring and evaluating AI systems, and implementing transparency in decision-making processes.

Furthermore, privacy and data protection are paramount when incorporating AI into your daily routine. AI algorithms often rely on personal data to function effectively, and it is essential to ensure that this data is handled with the utmost care and in compliance with privacy regulations. Users should be aware of the data being collected, how it is being used, and have control over their own data. Being mindful of the privacy settings of AI-powered applications and services and opting for providers with strong data protection measures can help safeguard personal information.

Another aspect of ethical AI usage is addressing the potential impact on jobs and the workforce. While AI has the potential to automate certain tasks, it is crucial to ensure that this technology is used to augment human capabilities rather than replace them entirely. This can be achieved by promoting AI literacy and upskilling programs that enable individuals to adapt to the changing job landscape. Additionally, companies should embrace responsible AI practices by actively creating new roles and opportunities in AI-related fields.

Lastly, accountability and transparency are vital in ensuring ethical AI usage. Users should have access to information about how AI systems make decisions and understand the reasoning behind those decisions. Engaging in open dialogues with AI developers and providers, as well as advocating for regulations that promote transparency, can contribute to a more responsible and ethical AI ecosystem.

In conclusion, incorporating AI into our daily routines requires a conscious effort to ensure ethical usage. By addressing biases, prioritizing privacy and data protection, considering the impact on jobs, and promoting transparency, we can unlock the power of AI while upholding ethical principles. As AI continues to evolve, it is essential for the general public to stay informed, engage in discussions, and actively participate in shaping the future of AI for the benefit of all.

Promoting Diversity and Inclusion in AI Systems

In recent years, artificial intelligence (AI) has become an integral part of our daily lives, transforming the way we work, communicate, and even make decisions. As AI continues to advance, it is crucial that we address the potential biases and inequalities that can arise within these systems. This subchapter will explore the importance of promoting diversity and inclusion in AI systems and provide practical strategies for incorporating AI into your daily routine while ensuring fairness and equality.

Diversity and inclusion are vital components of AI systems, as they can help mitigate biases and ensure that the technology serves the needs of all individuals. AI algorithms are often trained on large datasets that may inadvertently reflect societal biases, resulting in biased outcomes. For instance, facial recognition technology has been found to have higher error rates for women and people with darker skin tones. To combat these biases, it is essential to promote diversity both in the development teams creating AI systems and in the datasets used to train these algorithms.

One way to promote diversity is by encouraging a multidisciplinary approach to AI development. By involving individuals from diverse backgrounds, such as different ethnicities, genders, and cultures, we can incorporate a range of perspectives and experiences into the AI systems. This can help identify and address biases that may otherwise go unnoticed.

Additionally, it is vital to ensure that the datasets used to train AI systems are diverse and representative of the population they aim to serve. This means including individuals from different races, genders, ages, and socioeconomic backgrounds. By doing so, we can reduce the risk of biased outcomes and make AI systems more inclusive.

As a general public audience interested in incorporating AI into your daily routine, you can also play a vital role in promoting diversity and inclusion. By being aware of potential biases in AI systems, you can make informed choices about the technologies you use. Stay informed about the latest developments in AI and its impact on society, and support initiatives that prioritize diversity and inclusion in AI development.

In conclusion, promoting diversity and inclusion in AI systems is crucial for creating fair and equitable technology. By encouraging diversity in development teams, ensuring diverse datasets, and staying informed as users, we can play an active role in shaping AI systems that serve the needs of all individuals. Let us unlock the power of AI while striving for a future where technology is inclusive, unbiased, and beneficial for everyone.

Addressing Bias and Discrimination in AI

Artificial Intelligence (AI) has become an integral part of our daily lives, impacting various aspects of society. From personalized recommendations to autonomous vehicles, AI is transforming the way we live, work, and interact. However, despite its immense potential, there is growing concern about bias and discrimination within AI systems. In this subchapter, we will explore the importance of addressing these issues and provide practical guidance on how to incorporate AI into your daily routine while minimizing bias.

AI systems are only as good as the data they are trained on. Bias can inadvertently be introduced when the training data is not diverse or representative of the real world. This can lead to discriminatory outcomes, perpetuating existing societal biases and marginalizing certain groups. It is crucial to recognize and address these biases to ensure fairness and inclusivity in AI applications.

One of the key steps in addressing bias is to promote diversity in the teams developing AI systems. By including individuals with diverse backgrounds and perspectives, we can identify and mitigate biases that may otherwise go unnoticed. Additionally, it is essential to establish clear guidelines and ethical frameworks for AI development to ensure accountability and transparency.

Another approach to addressing bias in AI is through the use of data preprocessing techniques. These techniques involve carefully examining and cleaning the training data to identify and remove any biased patterns. Furthermore, ongoing monitoring and evaluation of AI systems can help detect and rectify bias that may arise due to changes in societal norms or new data inputs.

As a general public user of AI, there are steps you can take to minimize the impact of biased AI systems in your daily routine. Firstly, be aware of the limitations and potential biases of the AI tools you use. Understand that AI systems are not infallible and can make mistakes. By critically evaluating the outputs and being mindful of potential biases, you can make more informed decisions.

Additionally, supporting initiatives that advocate for diversity and inclusion in AI development can have a significant impact. By demanding diversity in the teams creating AI systems, we can ensure that different perspectives are taken into account and biases are actively addressed.

In conclusion, while AI has the power to revolutionize our lives, it is crucial to address bias and discrimination within these systems. By promoting diversity in AI development teams, implementing ethical frameworks, and actively monitoring for biases, we can work towards creating fair and inclusive AI systems. As general public users, being aware of the limitations of AI and supporting initiatives for diversity can contribute to a more equitable AI-powered future.

Designing AI for the Benefit of Humanity

In recent years, artificial intelligence (AI) has emerged as a transformative technology that has the potential to revolutionize various aspects of our lives. From virtual assistants to autonomous vehicles, AI is becoming increasingly integrated into our daily routines. However, as AI continues to advance, it is crucial to ensure that it is designed and utilized for the benefit of humanity. This subchapter explores the principles and considerations for designing AI systems that align with our values and contribute positively to our lives.

First and foremost, designing AI for the benefit of humanity requires ethical considerations. AI should be developed with a strong emphasis on privacy, transparency, and accountability. It is essential to protect user data and ensure that AI systems are transparent about their decision-making processes. By prioritizing these ethical principles, we can foster trust and confidence in AI technology, enabling a seamless integration into our daily routines.

Furthermore, AI should be designed to augment human capabilities rather than replace them. The goal is to create AI systems that work alongside us, assisting and enhancing our abilities. Whether it is in healthcare, education, or productivity, AI can provide valuable insights and support, enabling us to make more informed decisions and achieve better outcomes. By incorporating AI into our daily routines, we can leverage its power to simplify tasks, increase efficiency, and unlock new opportunities.

However, it is also important to recognize the potential societal impact of AI. Designing AI for the benefit of humanity requires careful consideration of the potential risks and biases associated with its implementation. AI systems must be designed to avoid reinforcing existing biases or perpetuating discrimination. It is essential to ensure fairness, inclusivity, and diversity in the data sets used to train AI models, as well as continuous monitoring to identify and mitigate any unintended consequences that may arise.

In conclusion, incorporating AI into our daily routines can bring numerous benefits, but it is crucial to design AI systems that prioritize the well-being of humanity. By adhering to ethical principles, focusing on augmentation rather than replacement, and addressing the potential societal impact, we can unlock the true power of AI while safeguarding our values. It is through a collective effort of individuals, organizations, and policymakers that we can shape the future of AI technology, ensuring its positive impact on our lives and society as a whole.

Chapter 9: Conclusion

Recap of Key Takeaways

Throughout this book, "Unlocking the Power of AI: A Practical Guide for Everyone," we have explored the fascinating world of artificial intelligence and how it can be incorporated into our daily routines. As a general audience seeking to harness the potential of AI, it is essential to recap the key takeaways from our journey so far.

First and foremost, we have learned that AI is not just a concept confined to science fiction movies; it is a real and powerful tool that can enhance our lives in numerous ways. From voice assistants like Siri and Alexa to personalized recommendations on streaming platforms, AI is all around us, making our lives more convenient and efficient.

We have also discovered that AI is not solely reserved for tech experts or scientists. With advancements in technology, AI is becoming increasingly accessible to the general public. Embracing AI does not require complex technical knowledge; rather, it necessitates an understanding of its potential and the willingness to explore its applications.

One important takeaway is the impact of AI on various aspects of our lives. From healthcare to education, AI has the potential to revolutionize industries and improve the quality of services we receive. AI-powered healthcare systems can help diagnose diseases accurately and efficiently, while AI-driven personalized learning platforms can make education more effective and tailored to individual needs.

Furthermore, we have identified ways to incorporate AI into our daily routines. From using smart home devices to automate tasks and increase energy efficiency to utilizing AI-powered health and fitness apps that track our progress and provide personalized recommendations, there are numerous ways for the general public to integrate AI seamlessly into their lives.

Importantly, it is crucial to address potential concerns and ethical considerations surrounding AI. We must ensure that AI systems are transparent, fair, and unbiased, and that they respect privacy and security. Understanding the limitations and potential risks of AI is key to using it responsibly and effectively.

In conclusion, unlocking the power of AI is not an exclusive privilege; it is a journey that anyone can embark upon. By recapitulating the key takeaways from this book, we have gained an understanding of AI's potential, its impact on our daily lives, and how we can incorporate it into our routines. The future is bright, and by embracing AI, we can unlock a world of possibilities.

Encouragement for Further Exploration of AI

Artificial Intelligence (AI) has become an integral part of our lives, revolutionizing the way we live, work, and interact. From voice assistants like Siri and Alexa to personalized recommendations on streaming platforms, AI has seamlessly integrated into our daily routines. However, there is much more to AI than meets the eye. In this subchapter, we encourage you, the general public, to further explore the vast potential of AI and discover how you can incorporate it into your daily routine.

AI is not limited to the realm of tech giants or researchers in labs. It is accessible to everyone, and understanding its capabilities can empower you to leverage its power in your personal and professional life. By embracing AI, you can enhance your productivity, make informed decisions, and unlock new opportunities.

One way to incorporate AI into your daily routine is by utilizing smart home devices. These devices, such as smart thermostats and lighting systems, can learn your preferences and adjust settings accordingly, ensuring optimal comfort while saving energy. Additionally, AI-powered virtual assistants can help manage your schedules, set reminders, and even provide personalized recommendations based on your preferences and habits.

Beyond personal convenience, AI can also aid in education and personal growth. Online learning platforms equipped with AI algorithms can provide personalized recommendations for courses and resources tailored to your specific interests and skillset. Learning becomes more efficient and enjoyable when AI assists in curating content that matches your learning style and goals.

Moreover, AI plays a crucial role in healthcare. From early disease detection to assisting in complex surgeries, AI algorithms can analyze vast amounts of data, helping doctors make more accurate diagnoses and providing personalized treatment plans. Keeping abreast of AI advancements in healthcare can empower you to take control of your well-being and make informed decisions regarding your health.

Lastly, AI can be a powerful tool for creativity and artistic expression. With AI-driven tools, you can create and edit stunning visual designs, compose music, or even write poetry. These technologies can act as your creative collaborators, offering suggestions and enhancing your artistic abilities.

In conclusion, AI is not just a distant concept; it is a practical tool that can enhance various aspects of your daily routine. By exploring the potential of AI, you can unlock new opportunities for personal and professional growth, improve your well-being, and unleash your creativity. Embrace the power of AI and witness the transformative impact it can have on your life.

Final Thoughts on the Power of AI in Transforming Lives

As we conclude this journey into the world of artificial intelligence (AI), it is essential to reflect on the profound impact this technology has had on transforming lives across various domains. AI is no longer limited to the realm of science fiction; it has become an integral part of our daily lives, revolutionizing the way we work, communicate, and even relax.

Incorporating AI into our daily routines has become increasingly accessible, thanks to the development of user-friendly applications and devices. From voice assistants like Siri and Alexa to personalized recommendations on streaming platforms, AI has seamlessly integrated into our lives, making tasks more efficient and enjoyable.

One of the most significant areas where AI has made a remarkable difference is in healthcare. With the ability to analyze vast amounts of data, AI has helped doctors in the diagnosis and treatment of diseases, leading to improved patient outcomes. Machine learning algorithms can identify patterns that humans might miss, allowing for early detection of conditions and the development of targeted treatment plans.

AI has also played a pivotal role in enhancing our productivity. From smart calendars that assist in scheduling tasks to virtual personal assistants that automate routine activities, AI has become a valuable tool in managing our busy lives. By taking care of repetitive or time-consuming tasks, AI frees up our time and energy, enabling us to focus on more important matters.

Moreover, AI has revolutionized the way we communicate and connect with others. Natural language processing algorithms enable real-time language translation, breaking down barriers and fostering global communication. Social media platforms leverage AI to curate personalized content, keeping us engaged and connected with the world around us.

However, as we embrace the power of AI, it is crucial to be mindful of ethical considerations and potential risks. Safeguarding privacy and ensuring transparency in AI algorithms are essential to prevent misuse and discrimination. As users, we must educate ourselves about the limitations and biases of AI systems to make informed decisions.

In conclusion, the power of AI in transforming lives is undeniable. By incorporating AI into our daily routines, we can streamline tasks, improve healthcare outcomes, enhance productivity, and foster global connectivity. As the field continues to evolve, it is up to us, the general public, to embrace AI responsibly and harness its potential to create a better future for all.